STANDARD LOAN

Unless recalled by another Reader
This item may be borrowed for

FOUR WEEKS

To renew, telephone:
01243 816089 (Bishop Otter)
01243 812099 (Bognor Regis)

£2.50

PERFECT PIGS

❧An Introduction to Manners❧

Marc Brown and Stephen Krensky

Collins

For the sow sisters -
Colleen and Kim

© Copyright 1983 Marc Brown and Stephen Krensky
ISBN 0 00 195623 X (hardback)
ISBN 0 00 195624 8 (paperback)
First published in the United Kingdom by
William Collins Sons and Co Ltd 1984
Printed and bound in Hong Kong
by South China Printing Co

Contents

At All Times   4
Around the House   6
With Your Family   8
On the Telephone   10
During Meals   12
With Pets   16
Giving a Party   18
Going to a Party   20
With Friends   22
At School   24
During Games   26
In Public Places   28

At All Times

Say "Please" when you ask for something . . .

and "Thank you" when you get it.

Think about and respect the feelings of everyone.

Clean up after yourself.

Take care of the property of others, as well as your own.

Remember that you can't always get your own way.

5

Around the House

Wipe your feet before coming inside.

Knock on the door before entering a room.

Play quietly if someone is sleeping.

NEATNESS AND CONSIDERATION ARE MY TRADEMARKS.

7

With Your Family

Ask to borrow things,
and return them when you're done.

Let others know you care about them.

Use words to solve arguments
instead of fighting.

8

Help out with chores.

On the Telephone

When making a call, give your name, then ask for the person you wish to speak to.

HELLO, THIS IS AGENT X. MAY I SPEAK TO AGENT Y?

When answering a call . . .

JUST A MINUTE, PLEASE. I'LL GET HER.

Don't call friends too early in the morning . . .
or too late at night.

When someone can't come to the
phone . . .

11

During Meals

Wash your hands before eating.

Ask politely for food that you can't reach.

When you sit down, put your napkin on your lap.
Use it to wipe your hands and mouth.

Cut your food into bite-size pieces.

Don't play with your food.

Don't talk with your mouth full.

ENOUGH TALK. WHEN DO WE EAT?

Use the right utensil or dish.

Be willing to try new foods.

Ask to be excused before leaving the table.

AND WHEN I'M DONE,

I ALWAYS HELP CLEAR THE TABLE.

15

With Pets

Train your pet to be friendly, but not too friendly.

16

Teach pets to play only with their own toys.

Don't feed pets during family meals.

Walk your pet on a lead.

Remember that a pet has feelings, too.

AND DON'T FORGET, A CLEAN PET IS A HAPPY PET.

17

Giving a Party

Send out your invitations at least a week ahead.

Introduce your guests to one another.

I'M VERY GOOD AT DOING DECORATIONS.

Offer refreshments to others before eating them yourself.

Spend some time with every guest.

When receiving presents, remember it's the thought that counts.

19

Going to a Party

Let the hosts know that you're coming so they can plan to include you.

Shake hands when meeting someone.

When choosing gifts, think of what others would like, not of what you would want.

Offer to help clean up.

Thank your host for inviting you.

WHAT DO YOU MEAN I WASN'T INVITED?

21

With Friends

Don't keep them waiting.

Share your toys.

I HAD A FRIEND ONCE... NO, MAYBE TWICE.

22

Don't make fun of others.

Help friends when they need you.

Be a good listener, and share your own ideas, too.

23

At School

Pay attention to your teacher.

Wait your turn to speak.

Make new children feel at home.

Take turns in the playground.

Walk, don't run, in the corridors.

I LIKE SCHOOL. WHAT MAKES YOU ASK?

25

During Games

Always obey the rules.

2-4-6-8 WHO DO WE OBLITERATE?

Don't lose your temper.

26

Be a good sport.

In Public Places

Give your seat to someone who needs it more than you do.

Wait patiently in queues.

Don't talk loudly or disturb others.

Hold a door open for anybody behind you.

Put litter in rubbish bins.

29

32